HOW TO LOOK AFTER YOUR
HAMSTER

A PRACTICAL GUIDE TO CARING FOR YOUR PET, IN STEP-BY-STEP PHOTOGRAPHS

DAVID ALDERTON

ARMADILLO

Introduction

Having a pet hamster is great fun. But before you get a hamster, ask yourself – do you have time to look after a pet? Hamsters must be fed and given clean water every day. You will also need to clean out your hamster's home twice a week and you should wash the home every two weeks. Then, you must remember to buy all the things that your hamster needs, such as its food and bedding. You will also have to spend time making friends with your hamster and playing with it for a few minutes each evening.

You'll need to think about where you can put your hamster's home.

You can buy special hamster food from a pet store or supermarket.

A caring owner

It is not difficult to care for a hamster, and you will be able to do this on your own most of the time, but sometimes you will need help from an adult. Hamsters are much easier to look after than some pets, because they live indoors and do not need to be taken out for walks. It takes only a few minutes each day to give your hamster food and water, and even cleaning out the cage takes less than 10 minutes.

A family pet

Hamsters can become special pets for everyone in the family. If you let other people help you look after your hamster, this will mean less work for you! Sharing your pet like this is actually a good idea, because other members of your family will know how to look after your pet if you are away, without you having to tell them. Your hamster will also be familiar with them, and so will not miss you as much.

Looking after a hamster can be fun for all the family.

Taming your hamster will be fun. Take good care not to be bitten though!

A happy home

Even if you live in an apartment, where you couldn't have a dog, a hamster will be perfectly happy. Hamsters are quiet and won't disturb your neighbours. They sleep through the daytime and wake up in the early evening, when you get home from school. This means your hamster will not be lonely when you leave it on its own during the day.

Don't cramp your pet in a small home. A cage this size will not be big enough for your hamster to run. It is also better to use a closed wheel, as this is safer.

What is a hamster?

Hamsters are small furry animals with short tails. There are sixteen different types of wild hamster in the world. They live in the Middle East and other parts of Europe and Asia. The largest is as big as a small rabbit, while the smallest fits into the palm of your hand. Only a few types of hamster can be kept as pets.

Hamsters are part of the mammal family, as they have warm blood and a hairy body.

Hamsters are mammals

All hamsters are part of the big group of animals called mammals. The mother hamster has babies that she feeds and looks after until they are able to take care of themselves. Hamsters are also members of the rodent family. Many hamsters come from areas where it is very hot during the day and then becomes very cold at night. They are covered in hair which helps to keep them warm.

The rodent family

Rats and mice, as well as guinea pigs and gerbils, are the hamster's closest relatives. These animals are all rodents. One thing that rodents have in common is their teeth. The teeth at the front of the mouth, called incisors, are very sharp and strong, which allows rodents to gnaw their food. Because a hamster's teeth are worn down by gnawing, they continue to grow throughout its life, unlike our teeth.

Hamster babies grow up fast. By the age of three months they are fully grown.

Night animals

Hamsters sleep during the day, coming out of their burrows at night when they are harder to see. In the wild, this helps to protect them from being caught for food by other animals. Being awake through the night, hamsters are often described as nocturnal animals. They have keen senses that help them to find their way in the dark.

Hamsters are nocturnal and they will be happy to be left alone during the daytime.

A furry coat helps to keep the hamster warm.

Large ears allow hamsters to hear faint sounds clearly.

Hamsters have large eyes but they cannot see very well in daylight.

Strong back legs can support the hamster's weight when it sits up.

The hamster uses its front paws just like hands, to pick up and hold its food.

Whiskers are long, thick hairs which hamsters use to find their way around in the dark.

By sniffing around, hamsters can find food and discover if other hamsters have been in the area.

Hamster varieties

Most people are familiar with short-haired Syrian hamsters, which used to always have golden coats, but these are not the only hamsters that make good pets. People have kept hamsters for many years, so all pet hamster varieties are friendly, unlike wild hamsters, which are shy of people. Pet hamsters occur in many different colorations now, so there is a wider range to choose from. Hamsters can be long- or short-haired, and some have shiny coats too.

Short-haired Syrian hamsters

Most pet hamsters are short-haired Syrian hamsters, named after Syria, the country they come from. They have been bred in many shades, including white, cream and grey.

This is the natural coat of Syrian hamsters in the wild, and is known as golden.

Long-haired Syrian hamsters

Hamsters with long coats are sometimes called Angoras and they need much more grooming than hamsters with short coats. At first, when babies, Angoras have quite short fur.

Long-haired hamsters have trailing fur, especially on the back of their bodies.

Syrian varieties

Not all hamsters are one shade. The popular tortoiseshell hamster has red and black fur. There are also chocolate and black hamsters, as well as banded hamsters, which are white mixed with another shade.

Tortoiseshells have a mixed coloration.

Dwarf Russian hamsters

These hamsters are smaller than Syrian hamsters and are more friendly towards each other. There are two types of dwarf Russian hamster. One is known as Campbell's and the other is called Winter White. They all have a dark line running down their backs.

Campbell's dwarf Russian hamsters are now being bred in different shades, just as with Syrians.

The Winter White hamster grows white fur in the winter. This helps it to hide in the snow in the wild.

Roborovski's hamsters

The smallest of the pet hamsters are called Roborovski's hamsters. They look rather like the dwarf Russian hamster, but have longer fur and are often not as friendly.

Chinese hamsters

Another type that is still rare are the Chinese hamsters, which have much longer tails than other hamsters. They also look a bit like dwarf Russian hamsters, although the Chinese is bigger.

The smallest hamsters to be kept as pets are the Roborovski's hamsters. They originally come from desert areas in China and Mongolia.

Small Chinese hamsters are becoming more popular as pets.

Choosing your hamster

It will be really exciting deciding which hamster to choose, but don't rush! You need to find a young hamster that is about four weeks old, because at this age, your new pet will be easier to tame. Hamsters are sold in many pet stores, but if you want a special type, you may have to go to a breeder. Ask an adult to search on the Internet for a hamster club in your area, so you can find a local breeder.

Syrian hamsters

It is very important that Syrian hamsters are kept on their own, because they will fight if put with another hamster. Remember that if you choose a Syrian hamster with markings on its coat, these will not change during your pet's life.

This Syrian hamster is alert and glowing with health. These are important factors to look for when choosing your pet.

Dwarf hamsters

You can keep two dwarf hamsters together, but buy them at the same time so they can settle down together. They will then be less likely to fight. Two females or two males will get on well, but avoid choosing one of each, because they will have babies, which you might not be able to look after properly.

Two dwarf hamsters can live together happily.

Male or female?

It is quite easy to tell whether an adult hamster is male or female, especially from a side view, without having to pick up your pet. Males have a step-like end to their bodies, while females have a much more rounded shape. Both make good pets.

You should ask the owner to pick up a young hamster to check if it is male or female. The gap between the openings on the underside of the body near the tail is bigger in males than females.

Adult male

Adult female

Picking a healthy hamster

Young hamsters are often quite sleepy, especially during the day. But once they wake up, they should be quite active and scamper around readily. When examining a hamster, check that the eyes are bright and even in size, and that the nose is clean. The hamster should feel relatively plump all over, and the fur must not be dirty under the tail.

Young hamsters are often sleepy. Try to choose your hamster later in the day, when it will be more awake and lively.

Taking your hamster home

A special plastic carrying container with air vents is ideal for taking your hamster home. You can use this later when you need somewhere to keep your pet while you clean out its home. If you don't have one, however, you can bring your pet home in a cardboard box, but watch that it doesn't chew its way out on the way home.

Line the base of the carrying box with some bedding, so that your new pet will be comfortable and can sleep on the journey home.

When you get home, put the carrying box on the floor of the cage and let your hamster come out on its own.

Your hamster's home

There are now many great ways in which you can house your hamster. Some are tunnel systems which you can clip together. These are rather like the tunnels in which hamsters live in the wild. But you may prefer a cage, so you can catch and handle your new pet more easily.

Bedding and wood shavings will make your hamster's home cosy.

Choosing a cage

Your hamster will need plenty of space to climb around and keep fit, so you should choose a large cage. There may be ladders for your hamster to scamper up, as well as platforms at different heights in taller cages. You will need to put wood shavings on the bottom of the cage for your hamster to burrow in.

Sleeping box

Give your hamster a box that it can use as a den for sleeping in. Your hamster will curl up here and rest during the day. Use special soft bedding that is safe for your pet. If the weather is very warm, your hamster might move its bed out of the sleeping box for a while.

Cover the floor of the cage with untreated softwood shavings or crushed barley straw.

Exercise wheel

Hamsters are very active, so an important addition to your hamster's cage is a playwheel. This should be solid rather than having open rungs because one of your pet's feet might slip through a gap and become stuck. Be sure that it fits well because wheels can be noisy. You may be kept awake by this at night if you keep your hamster's cage in your room.

Some wheels are free-standing, but others need to be fixed to the side of the cage.

Where to keep your hamster

- Out of cold breezes

- Not in front of a window or in direct sunlight

- Away from radiators

- In a position where its home cannot be knocked over

- Out of reach of dogs and cats

Feeding equipment

Fix a drinking bottle to the side of the cage using the special clip. Position it just off the ground where your hamster can reach it easily. Choose a sturdy food bowl that the hamster cannot tip over, and place this on the floor of the cage.

A drinking bottle will prevent the hamster's bedding becoming wet.

Choose a ceramic food bowl that your hamster cannot chew or knock over easily.

Feeding your hamster

Hamsters are very easy to feed, and you can buy special hamster food mixes at pet shops and some supermarkets. Hamsters eat a variety of different seeds and similar dried foods, but you should also offer your pet some fresh fruit or vegetables each day. Feed your hamster at the same time every day, for example in the early evening. Remember also to change the water at the same time.

Hamsters like to eat a mixture of different seeds.

A hamster's face looks very swollen when it has a peanut in its pouch.

Collecting food

When a hamster eats, it usually stuffs lots of food into its mouth very quickly, rather than nibbling it. Hamsters feed in this way so they are less likely to be caught by other animals in the wild. They are putting the food into big pouches inside their cheeks, rather than swallowing it. They then carry their food back to their home in these pouches.

When a hamster empties its pouches, it may use its front paws to ease the food out. If you look in your hamster's house, you are likely to find stored food here, which it will eat when it is hungry.

Always buy a hamster mix that has added vitamins and minerals.

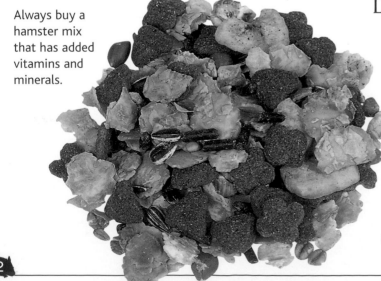

Dried food

Most hamster food consists of a mixture of different seeds. These may include flaked and whole maize, which is yellow in appearance, and flaked peas, which are pale green. Look out also for sunflower seeds, which are usually striped, and peanuts, which may have a papery red skin but are white underneath.

Some mixes also have vitamins and minerals added, to keep your hamster healthy. Hamsters generally eat about a tablespoon (7g) of dried food each day.

Fresh food

You can give your hamster all sorts of fresh foods, ranging from sweet apple to tangy tomato, as well as green vegetables such as cabbage. Wash all fresh food thoroughly. Only offer one piece of fruit or vegetable a day because it can cause a stomach upset if your hamster eats too much. Don't offer tomato or lettuce regularly, and only give a small piece each day. Every day, clear away fresh food from the day before. Check your hamster's bed for leftovers stored there.

Chop up the fresh food for your hamster into chunks, with adult help – but you don't need to bother peeling or coring it.

Special treats

Various treats are available for hamsters and you can give these to your pet occasionally, but do not use them in place of its regular seed mix. Remember that some foods are not suitable for hamsters and can make them ill. Don't give your hamster confectionery of any kind, particularly chocolate, or salted nuts or spicy food.

Some treats have hooks in them so you can hang them from the bars of the cage.

Handling

If you handle your hamster every day, it will quickly become used to being picked up. Don't try to pick it up straight away. Allow your hamster to settle down in its new surroundings for a day or so before you start to handle it. Then, talk to your pet and let it smell your hand so that it learns to trust you.

Don't get your hamster out of its cage until it is tame enough and you can handle it easily.

Feed your hamster some fresh food by hand so that it gets used to seeing your hand.

Picking up your pet

Hamsters have sharp teeth and can give you a painful bite if you do not handle them properly. A hamster's eyesight is not as good as ours, and your pet can be frightened easily if you try to pick it up without warning. Once your hamster is tame, it is unlikely to bite you.

1 Let your hamster sniff your hand, so it can smell your scent. It will soon learn that you will not hurt it.

2 Gently scoop your hamster up from beneath with the fingers of one hand.

3 Cup your hamster in both hands, remembering not to hold it tightly. Stroking your hamster just in front of the ears may calm it down.

Playing with your hamster

If you have a cat or dog, be sure that it is out of the room and the door is shut before you bring your hamster out of its cage. Otherwise your cat or dog might attack the hamster.

It is safest to sit down on the floor or on a chair or sofa, so that if your hamster does escape, it will only fall a short distance on to a cushion, and should not hurt itself.

Putting your pet back

Every time you put your hamster back in the cage, make sure that the door of the cage is properly closed afterwards. It can be very hard to find an escaped hamster in the home, and your pet could easily end up being caught by the cat.

Let your hamster walk from hand to hand, keeping your hands close to your chest. Sitting on the floor is safest in case your hamster should fall.

If your hamster escapes

The best time to search for a missing hamster is when it is getting dark, as your pet will be waking up and moving around then, so you might hear a noise.

You can set a special trap for your hamster if it is hungry. Place a ladder or ramp leading up to a bucket lined with soft bedding, and put some food in the bottom. Hopefully, when your hamster tries to reach the food, it will fall into the bucket and will not be able to get out. If you're lucky, you will find your pet asleep here in the morning.

You might be able to tempt your hamster out of hiding with some food.

Cleaning the cage

Every day you must remove any left-over fresh food your pet has hidden in its house. You will need to clean your hamster's cage completely twice a week. If it is kept in a dirty home, your hamster is more likely to fall ill and its cage will smell. Before you start cleaning the cage, catch your hamster and move it to its ventilated carrying box. It will be safe here until you are ready to put it back in its clean quarters.

Wear rubber gloves whenever you clear out your hamster's cage to keep your hands clean.

Dismantling the cage

The base of most cages comes off easily from the wire part above. All you then need is a plastic bag into which you can tip or scoop all the old cage floor covering and bedding.

Once the cage is clean, place a thick layer of shavings in the cage base.

Welcome home

Wipe the base with a piece of paper towel and then give your hamster a clean bed. Top up the food pot and change the water, line the base with untreated wood shavings and then replace the top section of the cage. Now, you can put your hamster back in the clean cage.

Disinfecting the cage

About once every two weeks, you should wash the cage, using a special disinfectant that is safe for hamsters. Empty the cage completely and then scrub the base and bars with a small brush.

Keep special scrubbing brushes and cloths that are just for cleaning your hamster's cage.

Rinsing the cage

After disinfecting the cage, you must rinse it very carefully and allow it to dry before putting it back together again. Wash plastic tubular cages in the same way.

Remember to wash your hands!

It is important that, when you have cleaned out your hamster's home or just handled your pet, you wash your own hands thoroughly with soap straight away. This should prevent any risk of you picking up an illness from your pet.

Water bottle

You also need to clean out the water bottle every week with a bottle brush and wash the food bowl before refilling it.

The easiest way to clean the water bottle thoroughly is to use a bottle brush.

Going away

Unfortunately, you will not be able to take your hamster on holiday with you unless you are staying at a friend's home just a short journey away by car. But it is usually not difficult to find someone who can look after your hamster. You could ask a friend to come to your house to feed your pet. Better still, you might be able to take your hamster, its cage and all of the necessary equipment round to your friend's house. Remember to clean the cage thoroughly before you go.

Ask a friend or an adult to help you carry your hamster's cage.

Always carry a hamster cage with your hands beneath it so that it does not fall apart.

Don't forget to take your hamster's carrying box so that your friend has somewhere to put your hamster when cleaning the cage.

Write a list of instructions

It is easier if you have a friend who has kept a hamster of their own and knows what to do. Even so, write out a list of the food your hamster needs, how much to give and when to feed it.

In case of emergency

Do not forget to leave details of where you can be contacted in an emergency, as well as the phone number of your vet, in case your hamster falls ill.

Keeping your hamster healthy

Most hamsters stay healthy throughout their lives if they are kept clean and well-fed. But if you think that your pet could be ill, then it is very important to contact a vet for advice as soon as possible. Hopefully, your hamster can then be treated and will get better quickly. Most hamsters live for about two or three years. As your hamster grows older, its coat is likely to become thinner. This is quite normal.

Checking claws

Hamster claws rarely become too long because they are worn down as the hamster climbs around its home, but you should check them regularly and get them trimmed if necessary.

Short-coated hamsters need little grooming, but you should brush hamsters with longer coats with a soft, clean toothbrush every few days to stop the fur becoming matted.

Caring for teeth

A hamster's teeth can become too long if it is not able to gnaw on hard surfaces and wear them down. This is why you should always put a chew, made of special wood, or a gnawing log in your hamster's cage, and possibly a mineral block, too.

If your hamster is having difficulty eating, it may be that its teeth need to be trimmed. Your vet will do this for you.

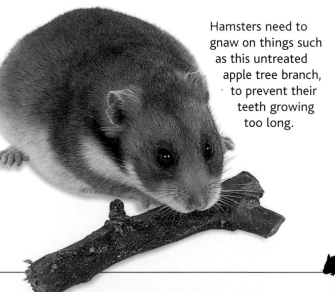

Hamsters need to gnaw on things such as this untreated apple tree branch, to prevent their teeth growing too long.

This edition is published by Armadillo, an imprint of Anness Publishing Ltd,
Blaby Road, Wigston, Leicestershire LE18 4SE; info@anness.com

www.annesspublishing.com

If you like the images in this book and would like to investigate using them for publishing,
promotions or advertising, please visit our website www.practicalpictures.com for more information.

Publisher: Joanna Lorenz
Editor: Sarah Uttridge
Designer: Linda Penny
Photographer: Bruce Tanner
Production Controller: Pirong Wang

The publishers would like to thank Grace Crissell, Eilish Main and Ben McLoughlin for appearing in this
book. Special thanks to David Baglin of the British Hamster Association for providing the hamsters.
Picture credit: NHPA/Daniel Heuclin 7br

PUBLISHER'S NOTE
Although the advice and information in this book are believed to be accurate and true at the time of
going to press, neither the authors nor the publisher can accept any legal responsibility or liability for any
errors or omissions that may have been made nor for any inaccuracies nor for any loss, harm or injury
that comes about from following instructions or advice in this book. If you are worried about your pet's
health, consult a veterinarian without delay.

Manufacturer: Anness Publishing Ltd, Blaby Road, Wigston, Leicestershire LE18 4SE, England
For Product Tracking go to: www.annesspublishing.com/tracking
Batch: 2729-22516-1127